World's Weirdest Critters

World's Weirdest Critters

by Mary Packard

illustrations by Leanne Franson

SCHOLASTIC INC.

New York   Toronto   London   Auckland   Sydney
Mexico City   New Delhi   Hong Kong   Buenos Aires

Developed by Nancy Hall, Inc.
Designed by R studio T
Cover design by Atif Toor
Photo research by Laura Miller

0-439-31456-9

12 11 10 9 8 7 6 5 4 3 2   1 2 3 4 5 6 / 0

Printed in the U.S.A.
First Scholastic printing, September 2001

Contents

World's
Weirdest
Critters

Introduction

Welcome to the weird and wonderful world of *Ripley's Believe It or Not!* Robert Ripley was the first millionaire cartoonist in history. A real-life "Indiana Jones," he traveled all over the world, tracking down amazing facts, oddities, and curiosities.

As a lifelong animal-lover, Ripley found the creatures he encountered in his travels especially appealing: the hairy frog from central Africa; the blood-sucking vampire bat from South America; and the duck-billed, web-footed platypus that would surely take first place in a contest for world's weirdest critter.

Ripley featured many of the animals he saw in the cartoons he drew for newspapers, and he started a file of fascinating animal facts that continues to grow to this day. As long as an animal is weird enough, it is guaranteed a place of honor in the files of Ripley's Believe It or Not!

In addition to the fabulous, the wild, and the exotic, Ripley was fascinated by the naturally occurring oddities in more common animals. He encountered such marvels as a dog with two noses, a mouse with two tails, a frog with six legs, and even a snake, a turtle, and a calf that each had the unfortunate distinction of being born with two heads.

World's Weirdest Critters is a dynamic collection of amazing animal facts straight from the archives of Ripley's Believe It or Not! Its pages are chock-full of wacky characters, like the bird that plucks hair from the heads of passersby to make a cozy nest, the dog that yodels instead of barking, the snake that can spray poisonous venom instead of biting, and the sea cucumber that regurgitates its insides when it's frightened.

You'll find all these incredible creatures and tons more in the pages of *World's Weirdest Critters*. While you're at it, you'll get a chance to test your critter smarts by answering the Who Am I? questions and completing the Ripley Brain Busters in each chapter. Then take the special Pop Quiz at the end of the book and use the scorecard to find out your Ripley's Rank. So get ready to meet some of the weirdest critters on the face of the earth. Their antics will amaze you.

Believe It!

CHAPTER 1

Mirror, Mirror on the Wall . . .

Who is the strangest of us all?

Some animals have such long tongues . . . they can use them to clean their ears . . .

Once called "camelopards" (a combination of the words *camel* and *leopard*), **giraffes** use their long prehensile (used-for-grabbing) tongues to pull leaves from trees. The average giraffe spends 16 to 20 hours a day collecting food, and eats up to 140 pounds of leaves.

. . . or to catch 30,000 ants in one day.

It's lucky that the **anteater** has such a long, sticky tongue because it doesn't have any teeth. The anteater's tongue can extend as far as two feet. Besides being sticky, it's covered with tiny spines that keep the ants from getting away.

Some animals have eyes as big as pizza pies . . .

Giant squid have the largest eyes of any animal. One reason their eyes are so big is that they are huge animals. A giant squid can weigh as much as 1,980 pounds! Scientists don't know for sure where giant squid live, but they suspect the squid live between 660 and 2,300 feet below the ocean's surface. And that's another reason for the squid to have such large eyes. They probably help the squid to use what little light there is at that depth to see.

Some have not two eyes, but three . . .

The **tuatara** has an extra eye on the top of its head. Scientists think that this eye is used as a light sensor to help the tuatara keep track of its time in the sun. It may also help with directions by keeping track of the sun's position in the sky.

Who Am I?

Like most animals, I have two eyes. It's the way I close my eyelids that's different. My eyes close from the bottom up.

Am I . . .

a. a snake?
b. a rabbit?
c. a gopher?
d. a turtle?

Some animals have sweat that looks like blood . . .

but it's really a kind of skin conditioner.

The **hippopotamus** needs this oily secretion because it spends much of the day lying in water. Without it, the hippo's skin would probably get all wrinkly like a prune. Scientists think that this oily substance also protects hippos from sunburn, and it may guard against infections as well.

Other animals don't perspire at all . . .

Because neither **tigers** nor **wolves** sweat, they need another means of cooling their body. So, just like dogs, they pant. The air rushing into the animal's mouth contacts the thin, wet skin inside and helps keep its temperature down.

Some frogs have hair . . .

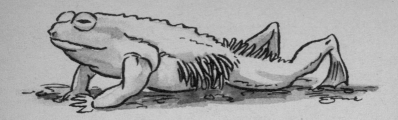

Certain **frogs** in the Democratic Republic of the Congo, a country in central Africa, look like they have hair. Their hips and thighs are covered with this hair, which can be as much as an inch long.

Some cats are bald . . .

The **sphynx,** a breed of hairless cat, has been recognized by the Cat Fanciers' Association since 1998. The first hairless cats were born as a result of natural genetic mutations. Then in the 1960s, people started to breed sphynx cats.

Who Am I?

I am a type of domestic cat that has no tail.

Am I . . .

a. a Manx?
b. a sphynx?
c. a Persian?
d. a Siamese?

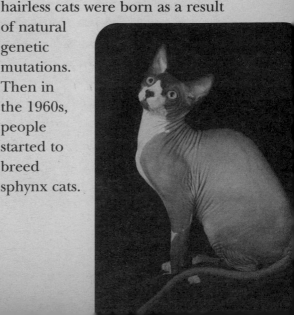

Some birds have stubs for wings . . .

Because its wings are so small, the **kiwi** (see color insert) cannot fly. Named for its call, the kiwi is the national bird of New Zealand.

Some birds can't fly, but know how to bark . . .

The barking **cagou** is native to New Caledonia, an island in the western South Pacific that is about the size of New Jersey. The bird lives in the mountains and coastal rain forests. Once on the endangered list, the cagou is making a comeback because of a captive breeding program.

And some dogs don't bark—they yodel.

The **basenji**'s yodel ranges from a soft crow to a piercing scream. Originally from central Africa, the basenji is thought to be one of the oldest breeds of dog. No one is really sure why these dogs yodel. Some people think they do it when they are happy. Why do basenjis sound different from other breeds of dog? Perhaps it's because their voice box is in a different place.

Some body parts are good for resting . . .

Who Am I?

I use my tail as an umbrella, a sunshade, and a blanket.

Am I . . .

a. a peacock?
b. a squirrel?
c. a ferret?
d. a beaver?

The **Abyssinian ground hornbill**, a turkey-sized bird found in the dry savannas of parts of Africa, takes a rest by leaning on its beak. These birds can fly, but they prefer to walk, and they catch most of their food on the ground. Their diet includes lizards, tortoises, and small birds as well as some fruits and seeds.

And some are good for moving on ice . . .

The **walrus** can use its long tusks to pull itself out of the water and up onto the Arctic ice. Both male and female walruses have tusks. The tusks don't appear until the animal is about a year old, and they continue to grow for 15 years. The tusks of the male walrus grow longer than those of the female. They can be as long as 39 inches!

Some creatures have more parts than they need . . .

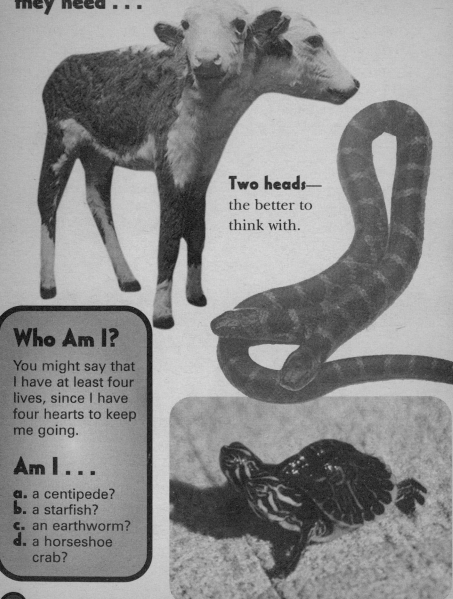

Two heads—
the better to think with.

Who Am I?

You might say that I have at least four lives, since I have four hearts to keep me going.

Am I . . .

a. a centipede?
b. a starfish?
c. an earthworm?
d. a horseshoe crab?

Two tails— the better to scare with.

Two noses—the better to smell with.

Six legs—the better to leap with.

While some are missing a few . . .

Gets by with a little help from its friends . . .

Missing its front legs when it was born, this pony needed some support to get around.

Wins more attention this way . . .

This strange-looking chicken was born without a beak.

Short on legs, long on attitude . . .

Although it had no hips or hind legs, this puppy could run almost as fast as a normal four-legged pup.

Others have parts that keep on growing.

Crocodiles continue to grow replacement teeth for as long as they live. They can grow as many as 3,000 teeth over the course of their lives. That's a lot to smile about!

Before winter, the **ruffed grouse** grows special snowshoes. A fringe on each toe prevents it from sinking into the snow. These fringes are probably one of the reasons that grouse thrive during severe winters. Found throughout North America, grouse prefer the aspen forests around the Great Lakes.

Who Am I?

One of my eyes has 13,000 lenses and 13,000 nerve rods. Yet if I should happen to lose one, I don't have to worry. I'll simply grow a new one.

Am I . . .

a. a human?
b. an ant?
c. a lobster?
d. a honeybee?

And some animals look all mixed up . . .

The **okapi** has striped legs like a zebra, a head like a giraffe, a neck like a horse, a body like an antelope, a tail like an ox, and a blue-black tongue that measures two feet long. Okapis, which are relatives of the giraffe, live in the rain forests of central Africa.

The **aardvark** has the body of a giant, hump-backed rat with the head of an anteater, the snout of a pig, the ears of a bear, the thick, powerful tail of a kangaroo, the claws of a tiger, and a flat tongue that's one and a half feet long!

Who Am I?

I produce venom like a snake. I'm a mammal, but I lay eggs like a bird. I have the bill and feet of a duck, and the tail of a beaver.

Am I . . .

a. an armadillo?
b. an aardvark?
c. a Tasmanian devil?
d. a platypus?

Ripley's Believe It or Not! Brain Buster

Ready to test your knowledge of the mind-blowingly bizarre, the super-strange, and the amazingly unbelievable?

The Ripley files are packed with info that's too out-there to believe. Each shocking oddity proves that truth is stranger than fiction. But it takes a keen eye, a sharp mind, and good instincts to spot the difference. Are you up for the challenge?

Each Ripley's Brain Buster contains a group of four unbelievable oddities. In each group of oddities only **ONE** is **FALSE**. Read each extraordinary entry and circle whether you **Believe It!** or **Not!** And if you think you can handle it, take on the bonus question in each section. Then, flip to the end of the book where you'll find a place to keep track of your score and rate your skills.

Which is stranger, fact or fiction? Can you tell? Check out this Ripley's Brain Buster. Remember, only one entry is false.

a. A mouse has more bones in its body than a human.

Believe It!   **Not!**

b. A single beaver can chomp down a tree five inches in diameter in only three minutes.

Believe It!   **Not!**

c. In addition to the ability to turn its head 180 degrees, an owl can fly upside down and backward.

Believe It!   **Not!**

d. A headless chicken laid an egg in Elizabethtown, Kentucky.

Believe It!   **Not!**

• •

BONUS QUESTION

Why was a Labrador retriever named Endel declared Dog of the Millennium by a dog food company?

a. Endel can pick up items from supermarket shelves, withdraw money from the ATM, and load and unload the washer and dryer. After he was injured during the Gulf War, Endel's owner worked out a special sign language with the dog. All he has to do is tap the top of his head, touch his cheek, or rub his hands together, and Endel knows to fetch his hat, razor, or gloves.

b. Endel uses his heightened canine senses to detect earthquakes before they strike. Before a quake hit Seattle, Washington, in 2001, Endel refused to eat. When the quake struck, he managed to get his owner to safety before their entire house collapsed.

c. Endel guided every ship in and out of Hatteras Inlet, off the coast of North Carolina, from 1910 to 1912, by running up and down the shore with a large beacon in his mouth. He never lost a single vessel.

What's for Dinner?

CHAPTER 2

Some critters don't have to eat very often . . .

The **pheasant** can live for an entire month without eating. Ring-necked pheasants are found in the wild in much of the northern United States. These birds were brought to America from China in 1881.

Others eat as often as they can . . .

Some people believe that the **cormorant** eats twice its weight in fish every day, but recent studies show that it only eats about 25 percent of its body weight. That means a four-pound bird eats about a pound of fish a day. In many parts of the world, cormorants in captivity catch fish for the people who raise them. The birds are fitted with a special neck strap that prevents them from swallowing.

The **little brown bat** can eat more than 3,000 insects, including mosquitoes, in one night. Some hungry bats even consume 1,200 insects in one hour. Bats use echolocation, a kind of sonar, to find their prey.

Some critters are picky eaters . . .

The **Siberian brown bear**
eats only fish heads.

The **Siberian white-breasted
bear** throws away the fish
heads. It only eats the bodies.

Who Am I?

When I get very
hungry, I go hunting
for sheep.

Am I a type of . . .

a. parrot?
b. zebra?
c. hippopotamus?
d. elephant?

Others are not picky at all . . .

The **kiwi** eats its weight in worms. Unlike most birds, the kiwi's nostrils are at the end of its long, thin bill, which the bird uses to search the ground for its wriggly breakfast, lunch, and dinner.

Some creatures have a mighty thirst . . .

The **vampire bat** (*see color insert*), a small bat of South America and Mexico, drinks more than its own weight in blood every night.

The **hummingbird** drinks the nectar of 1,000 flowers each day. It needs to drink a lot because it uses up so much energy flying around. This bird can flap its wings 55 to 75 beats per second. If trapped indoors, a hummingbird can starve to death within one hour.

Other creatures don't drink much at all . . .

Except in times of drought, the **koala** gets all its fluids from the eucalyptus leaves it eats. Because their diet of leaves is so low in nutritional value, koalas sleep about 16 hours a day. Sometimes called a koala bear, this critter is not a bear at all, but a marsupial.

Some animals take teeny, tiny bites . . .

Even though its mouth is so large a human adult male can stand inside it, the **blue whale** doesn't swallow anything bigger than a shrimp. Instead of teeth, this whale has baleen, a series of plates that hang down from the upper jaw and act as strainers. To collect food, blue whales strain gallons and gallons of seawater every day. Their main food source is krill, which are tiny shrimp-like creatures. Because the blue whale is the world's largest mammal, measuring between 75 and 100 feet long and weighing as many as 110 tons, it may eat as much as four tons of krill a day.

Some work hard for every bite . . .

The **silvery gull** breaks the shells of snails and mussels by dropping them from great heights. The gull will drop a single shell as many times as it takes to shatter.

Who Am I?

I have a very big appetite. In fact, I often swallow fish that are larger than I am. It's a good thing that my stomach and gullet are so stretchable.

Am I . . .

a. a shark?
b. a blowfish?
c. a sea bass?
d. a pelican eel?

The **peregrine falcon** dives at its prey at speeds of over 200 miles an hour. Then it zooms under its victim, turns on its back, and catches the wounded prey in its claws.

Some critters swallow things whole . . .

The **secretary bird** can swallow a hen's egg without breaking the shell. In the wild, this bird typically eats snakes, lizards, tortoises, mice, smaller birds, and sometimes grasshoppers. It often swallows small prey whole and alive. This bird, which stands between three and four feet high and rarely flies, lives and hunts on the plains and grasslands of Africa. On farms, tame secretary birds keep the fields free of snakes.

Who Am I?

I leave the water and climb into the branches of high trees to search for food.

Am I a type of . . .

a. sea otter?
b. fish?
c. frog?
d. lobster?

A **sea snake** swallows the fish it eats whole. Because of its hinged jaw, this snake can open its mouth wide enough to swallow a fish more than twice the diameter of its own neck. Sea snakes measure three to five feet long and are found in the Indian and Pacific Oceans. Like its relative, the cobra, the sea snake's venom is poisonous to people as well as to its prey.

Leaping Lizards

The **frilled lizard** scares off predators by rearing up and unfolding its fierce-looking mantle.

The **tuatara**, found only in New Zealand, is often referred to as a living fossil because it looks exactly as it did 240 million years ago when it first appeared on Earth.

How does the **thorny devil**, a lizard that lives in the Australian desert, beat the heat? Dew collects on its skin, then runs through thousands of tiny grooves right into the lizard's mouth.

Creepy Crawlies

When being chased by a wasp, a trapdoor spider retreats into its burrow and lies down with its abdomen facing upward. The abdomen is too tough and leathery for a stinger to penetrate.

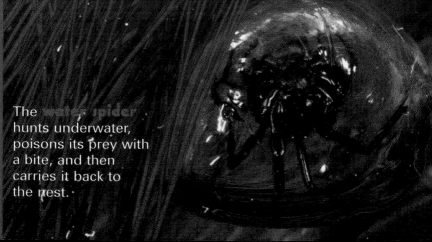

The water spider hunts underwater, poisons its prey with a bite, and then carries it back to the nest.

The **spicebush swallowtail** caterpillar scares off birds with the two black spots on its skin that look like a snake's eyes.

The wingspan of the **owl butterfly** can reach as wide as eight inches.

Wet and Wild

Although its brilliant blue rings make Australia's **blue-ringed octopus** look quite beautiful, no one should go near it. The poison from its bite eventually leads to respiratory failure.

Moray eels keep their mouths open to help them pump water over their gills to collect oxygen.

Parrot fish live in reefs and sleep in caves. Soon after dark, they wrap themselves in a mucous cocoon, or "blanket," that is formed in the mouth and passed backward in thick folds.

The **sea cucumber** is an ocean-dwelling animal that is found in both shallow and very deep water.

The **wolf fish** eats sea urchins and mussels, which it crushes with its incredibly strong teeth.

Marvelous Mammals

Also known as the earth pig, the **aardvark** uses its chisel-shaped claws to break open the hard clay nests of termites. Then it scoops up the termites with its sticky tongue.

Members of the mongoose family, **meerkats** are very social and live together in packs in the deserts of southern Africa.

In addition to its hairlessness, the **sphynx cat** is known for its playful disposition.

Vampire bats bite animals and people while they're sleeping, then lap up blood from the wounds.

Covered with scales, **pangolins** of Asia and Africa look like giant pinecones.

Shy rain forest dwellers, **okapis** are related to giraffes. But at five feet tall, they're from the short side of the family.

Flaky Flock

The **lyrebird** gets its name from the musical instrument it resembles. During courtship, the male spreads out its tail, which is shaped like an ancient Greek harp called a lyre.

Emus, large brown flightless birds found only in Australia, hiss, grunt, and utter loud booming calls.

Although the **kiwi** cannot fly, it can run very fast.

Each year during courting season, both male and female **puffins** grow an extra beak that drops off after they've found mates.

Some eat while swimming . . .

The **elephant seal** only eats when it is underwater. Male seals fast for up to three months at a time when they come on land to molt and to breed. Females also fast, but for less time. Even the

pups go for long periods without eating. After they are weaned and their mother leaves them, the pups stay on land for eight to ten weeks and don't eat a thing the whole time. During this period, they typically lose about one-third of their body weight.

Some eat upside down . . .

A **flamingo** eats with its head held upside down. It turns its long beak so that the bottom half faces the sky, while the top half is totally underwater. Thin slits on either side of the top of its bill act as strainers. They filter out sand, mud, and insects, while keeping in the mollusks that are the flamingo's favorite food.

Some creatures fish for their food . . .

The **osprey** is the only type of hawk that dives into the water to catch its prey. To find a good fishing location, the osprey watches other birds, noting what they've caught and their flight paths. Then it dives into the water, catches the fish it prefers, and tears it apart with its talons.

The **green-backed heron** catches insects to use as bait. It drops them on the water, then swoops down to devour the fish that rise to the bait.

Who Am I?

I live in the Pacific and Indian Oceans, but when I'm hungry, I climb trees to find my favorite food— coconuts.

Am I . . .

a. a lobster?
b. a crab?
c. a snail?
d. a sea lion?

While others hunt . . .

A **polar bear** can smell and locate prey at a distance of 20 miles. It often swims far from shore to reach the seals and walrus cubs it likes to eat. Polar bears will also eat shellfish and seabirds. In a pinch, they'll even settle for seaweed. On land, the polar bear's large furry paws act like snowshoes to help it silently stalk caribou when it's in the mood for an extra-hearty dinner.

A **coyote** can hear a mouse moving under a foot of snow. Also known as the prairie wolf, the coyote is valuable to farmers because it hunts small animals such as rabbits, mice, and gophers that can damage crops. Coyotes live in most of North America. They are adaptable animals and will eat just about anything that's available, including grasshoppers and blueberries.

Some fish like to go fishing . . .

The female **deep-sea anglerfish** has its own built-in fishing rod. The luminous, or glowing, bit of flesh at the end of her dorsal fin serves as bait to lure her prey close enough to be snapped up. The male anglerfish attaches himself to a female, then depends on her for survival.

The **scorpion fish** also uses its dorsal fin as a lure. When raised, the fin looks like a smaller fish. Medium-size fish are attracted to the fin—and before they know it, they end up as dinner for the scorpion fish.

While some fish venture onto land . . .

During times of drought, certain types of African **catfish** leave their ponds at night to travel to bigger ponds. These fish are able to breathe air and may crawl for miles in search of a new watery home.

Who Am I?

I catch mice by drowning them in the sea.

Am I . . .

a. a porpoise?
b. a clam?
c. an oyster?
d. a seal?

Some creatures trap what they eat . . .

The larva, or young, of the **sand runner** catches insects by digging a trap in the sand and plugging the opening with its body.

Instead of spinning a web, the **trapdoor spider** builds a burrow with a trapdoor. The burrow is about six inches long. The trapdoor is made of dirt and is attached to the side of the burrow with silk that the spider spins. The spider camouflages the 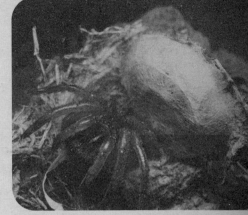 door with leaves, sticks, and small stones. Then it hides under the door, waiting for prey to come along. When the spider hears an insect on the other side, it jumps out, grabs the bug, and pulls it into the burrow.

Others like to shoot it . . .

The **archerfish**, a freshwater fish found in Asia and Australia, uses its long snout like a gun. It shoots at insects up to three feet away with jets of water, which cause the insects to fall where the archerfish can reach them.

Some critters wait for food to find them . . .

The **moray eel** curls up and hides in a hole or under coral until prey swims by. Then it attacks with lightning speed. This eel eats damselfish, cardinal fish, octopus—and even other eels.

While some find food on trees . . .

One of the **Hanuman langur**'s favorite foods is a fruit containing strychnine, a poison deadly to humans. Although they eat a variety of things, their diet is mostly leaves. A specially designed stomach helps these monkeys break down all the fiber. In India, some people feed Hanuman langurs because they consider them sacred to the monkey god.

Who Am I?

I have a very thick-walled throat and esophagus. It's a good thing, too. Otherwise I'd get splinters from the food I like to eat.

Am I . . .

a. a giant panda?
b. a woodchuck?
c. a beaver?
d. a termite?

Brain Buster

Bow-WOW! This doggy Brain Buster is doggone unbelievable! Are you ready to check out some bizarre canine behavior? Then take a shot at spotting which one of these Believe It! or Not! entries is false.

a. For three years a dog named Dorsey was the only mail carrier between Calico and Bismarck in California's Mojave Desert. It was a three-mile trip each way—and Dorsey always stayed on schedule.

Believe It!   **Not!**

b. Bonkie, an Irish setter belonging to Justin McClean of Cambridge, Massachusetts, graduated from Harvard University with a degree in The Science of Search and Rescue.

Believe It!   **Not!**

c. A former bomb-sniffing dog named George has been retrained to sniff out cancer in people. He has a higher success rate than X rays!

Believe It!   **Not!**

d. Fudge, a dog in England, swallowed a musical alarm watch. Every morning at 6:45, Fudge played a tune—like clockwork! The watch was successfully removed in an operation. You've got to shut off the alarm sometime!

Believe It!   **Not!**

BONUS QUESTION

What's so special about Bosco, a black Labrador retriever owned by Tim Stillman of Sunol, California?

a. Over the course of 11 years, Bosco has saved the lives of more than 30 people in this small town.

b. Bosco's been delivering newspapers and coupon circulars to the townspeople for over 16 years—without any human help.

c. Bosco was the mayor of this small community for more than eight years. He earned more votes than the two humans who ran against him for office!

Some animals' homes are hidden . . .

The male **wedge-tailed hornbill**, a large African bird, protects its mate and their eggs by hiding them in a hollow tree and plastering mud over the entrance. A tiny slit is left through which the hornbill passes food to its mate. The meals consist of food that he has swallowed and then regurgitated.

The **lion** protects its cubs in a lair hidden among rocks or in a cave. Lions usually live in rocky areas, sandy plains with thick bushes, or near streams that provide tall grasses among which to hide. The adaptable lions of the Masai Mara, an area of Kenya, actually climb trees and rest in their branches.

Others stand out . . .

Some **wasps** build a nest that stands out like a banner from a tree branch. The wasps make a paperlike substance by chewing on wood fibers. Then they use the mixture of fibers and saliva to build the nest. These wasps are sometimes called social wasps because, like bees, they live and work with a group of other wasps.

Some homes are delicate web sites . . .

The female **hummingbird** uses spiderwebs to help hold her tiny nest together. She also uses the fuzzy parts of cattails or dandelions to line the nest, and places lichen on the outside walls so that the nest looks like just a bump on the tree. Although this delicate structure typically measures only two inches across and two inches deep, it can take a hummingbird six to ten days to build it.

Who Am I?

The mail carriers stopped delivering the mail in my neighborhood until my babies grew up. That's because I attacked when they got too close to my nest.

Am I . . .

a. a wasp?
b. a mockingbird?
c. a bumblebee?
d. a bluejay?

Some have showers . . .

The **American dipper** often builds its globe-shaped nest in the spray of a waterfall. The mist from the waterfall keeps the outer layer of moss green. The inside, which is made of grass, stays relatively dry. Dippers use the same nests year after year. One nest has even been occupied by dippers for more than 100 years!

Some homes are quite large . . .

Built out of sticks, the nest of the **bald eagle** can weigh as much as two tons and measure nine feet across and 12 feet deep. Couples return to the same nest year after year.

While others are tiny . . .

One kind of cave-dwelling **swiftlet** doesn't use twigs to build its shelflike home. Instead, it constructs its small nest entirely from its saliva. Some people consider the nests of these small birds a delicacy and collect them to make bird's-nest soup.

Some homes come stocked with food . . .

The **solitary wasp**, which lives alone rather than in a hive, lays its eggs in a nest with paralyzed insects inside. The wasp collects the insects and stings them so they can't move. After the eggs hatch, the larvae (the young wingless wasps) eat the insects their parent has provided.

And others are equipped with air . . .

The **water spider** stocks its underwater nest with air by bringing it down in big bubbles from the surface. Tiny hairs on the spider's legs and body help it to carry the air bubbles. The spider's nest, which is made from silk that it spins, is where the creature eats.

Who Am I?

I always build my nest so that one end of it points to the north and the other to the south.

Am I a type of . . .

a. ant?
b. worm?
c. lizard?
d. toad?

Some critters
make nests out of leaves . . .

The **Australian sugar glider** bites off large leaves and carries them wrapped up in its tail. It uses the leaves to line its nest in the hollow of a tree. A type of opossum, the sugar glider, like a kangaroo, is a marsupial. This ten-inch critter sails through the air by stretching the membrane between its front and back legs and using it like a sail.

The **tailorbird**, a type of Asian thrush, uses its beak to poke holes in a leaf—then laces the leaf together with grass to make a cozy nest.

Others build their nests
with stones . . .

The **lamprey eel** carries heavy stones to construct its nest at the bottom of the sea. The nests of these eels can measure as much as three feet high and four feet around.

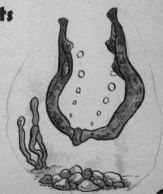

And some don't make nests at all . . .

The **puffin** lays its single egg in a burrow it digs near the coast. These seabirds of the Northern Hemisphere gather in large groups in the spring to lay their eggs. The parents take turns incubating the egg and feeding the puffling, which hatches in about six weeks.

Who Am I?

I build my mud nest in the shape of a ball. To hold it together, I plant seeds, so it soon looks like a tiny flower garden.

Am I a type of . . .

a. worm?
b. bird?
c. ant?
d. grasshopper?

Some live in high-rises . . .

Bank swallows dig burrows in the side of a cliff or a riverbank, creating bird "apartment buildings." Their tunnels can be up to three feet long. Colonies of bank swallows may contain as few as 12 pairs of birds or as many as several hundred. Bank swallows lay their eggs in the spring in many parts of North America.

Or have water views . . .

The female **pie-billed grebe** builds her nest in the form of a raft that she attaches to a reed so it won't float away.

Some work alone . . .

The male **satin bowerbird** attracts females with a nest that he has decorated with red berries, flowers, bits of colored cloth, and seashells.

Others have help . . .

The **hermit crab** lives inside its shell with a sea worm that keeps it clean. Hermit crabs don't grow their own shells, but use shells abandoned by other creatures on the ocean floor. When a hermit crab grows, it just moves into a bigger shell.

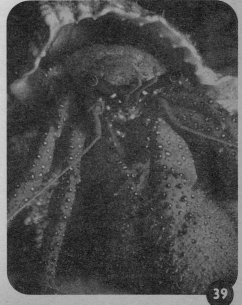

Who Am I?

Just the thought of building a nest makes me want to snooze. That's why I've perfected my imitation of a rattlesnake. One hiss and the squirrels run from home, leaving me a ready-made burrow to live in.

Am I . . .

a. a mole?
b. a prairie dog?
c. a ferret?
d. an owl?

And some work in construction crews . . .

The **agricultural ant** of Texas builds the colony's nest in an area of thick, tall grass after preparing a clearing and building a system of roads in all directions. This species of ant gets its name because it actually collects seeds, which are known as ant rice, and plants them to grow its own favorite grass.

Work it! These animals get down to business in the most unbelievable ways. In each Brain Buster, one Ripley's rarity is completely made up. Can you tell which one it is?

a. Isaac is a golden retriever that can add, subtract, multiply, and divide. He even does square roots! When Isaac was a puppy, his owner Gary Wimer started spending 20 minutes a day teaching the dog to count. Now, Wimer just asks Isaac what the square root of 36 is, and Isaac barks six times!

Believe It!   Not!

b. A parrot named Alex has been the subject of Irene Pepperberg's research at the University of Arizona for 22 years. Alex has a vocabulary of 100 words. He can also identify 50 different objects and sort them by color, shape, and texture. Research has proven that Alex doesn't just copy what he hears but actually processes information!

Believe It!   Not!

c. Snowcone is a singing leopard living in New York's Bronx Zoo. Snowcone can belt out the entire melody of "The Star-Spangled Banner" as well as the theme song from *Gilligan's Island*!

Believe It!   Not!

d. Suti, a 6,500-pound African elephant who lived at Chicago's Lincoln Park Zoo, used his trunk to make abstract paintings.

Believe It!   **Not!**

• •

BONUS QUESTION

Why does a miniature horse named Twinky need to wear little sneakers?

a. Twinky is a champion country line dancer. He's finished in first place in over 115 competitions and frequently performs at county fairs and festivals in his hometown of Elmwood, Illinois.

b. Twinky is a trained guide animal for the blind. He needs the traction to avoid slipping and sliding at the mall.

c. Twinky burned the bottom of his hooves while dragging his sleeping owner from a burning barn. The sneakers protect Twinky's sensitive hooves from rocks and debris on the ground.

Friends or Foes

Some critters help other kinds of critters . . .

The **parrot fish** (*see color insert*) balances vertically in the water while a school of smaller fish called **wrasses** use their pincerlike jaws to pick them clean of parasites.

The **Egyptian plover**, also known as the crocodile bird, picks and cleans the teeth of Nile crocodiles. These plovers eat insects and leeches, creatures that the crocodile is happy to do without. Egyptian plovers are found in several parts of Africa and in Asia.

Tickbirds, such as the **red-** or **yellow-billed oxpecker**, ride on the back of the rhinoceros. The bird eats ticks and other insects from the rhino's skin, so the rhino is less itchy. In addition to eliminating bugs, they serve as early warning systems for their four-legged friends. When predators approach, the tickbirds raise the alarm by squawking and flying away.

And some become quite attached to each other . . .

In 1986, a **moose** appeared on Larry Carrara's Vermont farm. The moose began to court one of Carrara's cows, a Hereford named Jessica. He walked in circles around her, rubbed his head against her, or just rested his neck across her back. He stayed with Jessica for 76 days.

Thousands of people came to visit this unlikely couple. After the moose left, Carrara and author Pat Wakefield wrote a book called *A Moose for Jessica*.

Who Am I?

I don't usually bond with cows, but if placed in the same pen, cattle will protect me from predators.

Am I . . .

a. a dog?
b. a sheep?
c. a cat?
d. a goose?

Other critters speak only to their own kind . . .

Honeybees communicate with a body language so subtle that only bees from the same geographical area can tell what it means. If a bee wants to tell its hive mates exactly where to find some tasty flowers, it does a kind of dance. The better the food source, the longer and more energetically the bee will dance.

Red-capped mangabeys, medium-size tree-dwelling African monkeys, communicate by using facial expressions. Mangabeys have white eyelids that are easily visible in the dim light of the forest. The white facial highlights enable these monkeys to "talk" to one another from quite a distance.

An **elephant** sends messages over long and short distances using a "secret code" of low-frequency sounds. The sounds the elephants make are quite loud, but because they are of such a low-frequency, humans cannot hear them. Other elephants can hear these low-frequency sounds from distances of more than five miles away.

Prairie dogs, a type of large, burrowing squirrel native to the western United States, identify one another by kissing. When two prairie dogs meet, they each press their teeth against the other's face. Some scientists believe that prairie dogs use touch, sounds, and body language to communicate with other prairie dogs from their own or neighboring colonies.

Who Am I?

The males of my species don't really like to fight. But if another male acts unfriendly, I act like a proud father and show him my baby. Then he forgets his threats and fusses over the baby.

Am I a type of . . .

a. manatee?
b. sea lion?
c. dolphin?
d. monkey?

The **elephant snout fish** communicates by sending out electrical signals. The electrical impulses that this freshwater fish sends out fill the water all around it. Changes in the current let the fish know what other kinds of fish are nearby.

Ermine, members of the weasel family that have long been prized for their beautiful white winter coat, mourn when one of their species dies. Ermine are native to northern areas of America and Europe.

Some critters like to be courted . . .

The female **Arctic tern** will not mate until her suitor brings her a gift. The male tern catches a fish and flies over the head of the female he is courting. If the female tern accepts his offering, she will rise up and fly with him. In the summer, Arctic terns breed in the Northern Hemisphere. Arctic terns make the longest migratory journey of any bird, flying as far away as Antarctica. Some of them travel as many as 20,000 miles a year.

And some have several mates . . .

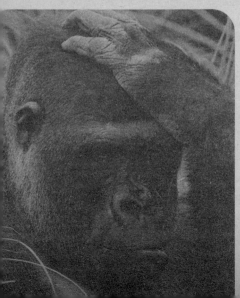

Gorillas live in bands of six or seven, made up of one dominant male and several females and young animals. In their natural habitat in western Africa, the male gorilla breeds with the females. When a young male gorilla in the band reaches maturity, he leaves and forms his own band.

Lions live in prides of between three and 30 individuals. The females in one pride are all related to one another. When the male cubs in the pride grow up, they leave the pride and travel with other males in a group called a coalition. A coalition takes over a pride of females. After two to four years, another male coalition kicks the males out and takes over the pride.

While others mate for life . . .

If a **crane**'s mate dies, it remains a loner for the rest of its life. Cranes are tall wading birds that look a lot like herons. There are 14 different kinds of cranes, and they live all over the globe except in South America.

The **lag goose**, sometimes called the gray-lag goose, also mates for life. Most domestic geese in Europe and America are descended from the European gray-lag goose.

Some critters are equipped for a fast getaway . . .

The **flying dragon** is equipped with a pair of "wings." These are actually folds of skin stretched over its long rib bones that allow it to "fly" from tree to tree. Like flying squirrels, however, these five-inch southeast Asian lizards don't really fly, but glide. They can glide as far as 150 feet.

Who Am I?

My mate likes to sing to me. I let him know which parts of his song I like by raising my wing in approval. My mate responds by repeating those parts I liked best.

Am I . . .

a. a cowbird?
b. a mockingbird?
c. a nightingale?
d. a canary?

Or pack anti-sonar devices . . .

Bats use their special sonar, called echolocation, to track down moths and other insects. But **tiger moths** can escape capture by sending out signals to warn the bat that it is about to land a terrible-tasting meal. Several other types of moths are also able to detect the bat's sonar and avoid getting eaten.

Others use scare tactics to get away . . .

The **frilled lizard** scares off predators by rearing up and unfolding its fierce-looking frill. With its frill down, the lizard looks like the bark that it sits on, and it is hard to spot. When a predator comes near, the lizard will first crouch down against the bark. If the predator continues, the lizard will rear up, open its mouth, and display its imposing frill. Sometimes it will hiss and jump forward to add to the frightening effect.

Who Am I?

I charge my prey at such great speeds they usually don't have a chance to escape. I am so ferocious, I've even been known to devour humans.

Am I . . .

a. a gorilla?
b. an elephant?
c. a komodo dragon?
d. a buffalo ?

Some creatures have bodyguards . . .

On their shells, **hermit crabs** carry anemones, whose stinging tentacles protect them from predators. When the crab moves to a new shell, sometimes the anemone does, too. In the wild, hermit crabs eat plants and other animals. Some people keep the land-dwelling species of hermit crab as pets.

Some use trickery . . .

The **California roadrunner** captures rattlesnakes by piling cactus spines around the snakes while they sleep. This desert bird, native to South America, Mexico, and the southwestern United States, is the state bird of New Mexico. When it runs, it raises its tail and lowers its head so that they are level with the horizon.

The **crested bellbird** fools predators by moving its voice from tree to tree like a ventriloquist. Bellbirds are found in wetland areas of Australia and in Venezuela.

The songs and cries of the **lyrebird** (*see color insert*) are imitations of other birds. This bird lives deep in the forests of Australia.

Some critters throw up . . .

When attacked, the **sea cucumber** defends itself by expelling its own digestive system. The attacker becomes entangled in it, and the sea cucumber goes free. Luckily, the sea cucumber, which lives on the seafloor, is able to regenerate its insides.

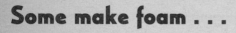

Some make foam . . .

The **hedgehog** eats poisonous toads, then froths at the mouth and licks toad toxins onto its spines to protect itself from predators. Sometimes, though, the hedgehog will just lick a live toad and then let it go. This critter curls up in a ball with its spines facing out whenever it feels threatened.

Who Am I?

Don't mess with me. I can secrete enough venom to kill seven people.

Am I a type of . . .

a. horned toad?
b. boa constrictor?
c. blowfish?
d. octopus?

Others make noise. . .

The roar of the **tiger** can be heard for a distance of two miles. This Asian cat is the largest member of the cat family, so it's not so surprising that its voice can carry. The average weight of a tiger is between 500 and 600 pounds.The largest tiger ever recorded was a male Siberian tiger that weighed in at 1,025 pounds!

And some power spray . . .

The **civet**, a catlike animal found in Africa and Asia, drives off its enemies with a foul-smelling spray. This spray is actually used in the manufacture of some perfumes. Pee-yew!

When pursued by a hawk, the **houbara bustard** sprays its foe's eyes and feathers with a thick sticky fluid that blinds and disables it. This desert bird was once common on the Arabian Peninsula and across Central Asia and Pakistan, but because of overhunting, the houbara bustard has become endangered.

Some creatures squirt blood . . .

The **horned toad** reacts to attack by squirting blood from its eyes as far as four feet. This lizard, the official state reptile of Texas, can measure up to five inches long. Its horns are actually scales on the sides and back of its head. When threatened, the horned toad will first flatten itself in hopes of not being seen. Then it will puff its body up to twice its normal size. Finally, the lizard will resort to its blood-squirting trick. It can squirt blood both forward and backward.

Who Am I?

Even after I have died, I can still slash and bite an attacker.

Am I . . .

a. an alligator?
b. a caiman?
c. a wolf?
d. a bobcat?

Stand on their heads . . .

The **stickleback** fish frightens off predators by standing on its head. There are a number of different kinds of sticklebacks. Some live in freshwater, some live in salt water, and some live in brackish waters, which are a mix of salt and fresh. The stickleback get its name from the spines on its back. Some people think sticklebacks may be killing off native fish in parts of the United States by eating their eggs.

Or wear protective gear . . .

The **sponge crab** cuts a piece of sponge and fits it perfectly over its back to make itself unappetizing to predators. This crab holds its sponge in place with its back pair of legs. Often sponge crabs also wear a coating of algae, which gives them further protection from the octopuses that like to eat them. If a sponge crab can't find a piece of sponge, it will use a piece of shell, a sea anemone, or even part of a tourist's flip-flop sandal.

The **porcupine** puffs up its quills, which makes it look quite unappetizing. If attacked, the porcupine will use its tail to drive the quills into its foe. Porcupine quills are painful and are hard to remove. The quills have barbs (little hooks) that point backward and tear the skin if you try to pull them out.

Some critters wear a disguise . . .

Large, thorny spines cover the body and tail of the **thorny devil**, helping it blend into its harsh desert home. The favorite food of this Australian lizard is ants, which it licks up one at a time with its sticky tongue.

Who Am I?

It would be hard for a predator to sneak up on me. That's because my eyes move independently of each other so I can look in two directions at the same time.

Am I . . .

a. a chameleon?
b. an owl?
c. a bat?
d. a hawk?

The **measuring worm**, which is actually the caterpillar of a moth, deceives predators with its camouflage. Its colors help it to blend in with the twigs of trees on which it feeds. Some types of measuring worms have little spikes that stick up and look just like tiny twigs. This caterpillar can also stand on one end and remain motionless. That way it looks even more like part of the tree.

Some join gangs . . .

Meerkats join together to fight a predator. They stand on their hind legs and move forward menacingly as if they were one fierce animal. When working with their gang—the name for a group of meerkats—they can scare off some of their major predators, including jackals and cobras.

Show off their high jumps . . .

Gazelles can leap high into the air to show a predator that it has been spotted and to try and discourage it from pursuit. This kind of jumping—straight up into the air— is known as "pronking."

Or simply kick . . .

An **ostrich** can kill a lion with one well-placed kick. This flightless bird is the largest bird in the world, and can grow up to eight feet tall, weigh 300 pounds, and run more than 40 miles per hour.

Some animals go undercover . . .

The **yellow-footed marsupial mouse**, which is also known as an antechinus, escapes the notice of flying predators by walking upside  down on a twig. Like other marsupials, the mother gives birth to tiny babies that live inside her pouch until they are big enough to move around on their own.

Spit stunning poison . . .

The **spitting cobra** of Africa can spray venom through an opening in the front of its fangs for several feet. Its venom can cause blindness.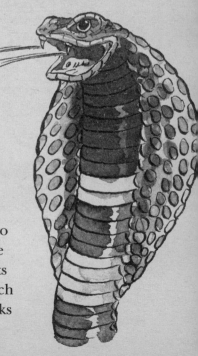

Show their sharp teeth . . .

The **wolf fish** (*see color insert*), has so vicious a bite that its teeth can leave marks on an iron anchor. Despite its fearsome jaws, these fish spend much of their time hiding among the rocks on the seafloor.

Curl into a ball . . .

When threatened, the **pangolin** (*see color insert*), which is also known as the spiny anteater, rolls itself up so tightly that three men pulling at its tail cannot straighten it out. The name "pangolin" comes from the Malay word that means "to roll."

Who Am I?

Other animals can tell how fierce I am by the length of my beard.

Am I . . .

a. an antelope?
b. a goat?
c. a bison?
d. a bull?

Do their best to hide . . .

The **solenodon** buries its head in the sand to escape detection by a predator. This ratlike, insect-eating creature is very rare. Found only in Haiti and Cuba, the nocturnal solenodon, a relative of moles and hedgehogs, lives in dense, humid forests and on the edges of plantations. Some scientists estimate that there may be fewer than 100 left in existence.

Develop magnificent eyesight . . .

The **giraffe**'s eyes protrude so far it can see in all directions without turning its head. This panoramic view allows it to spot a predator approaching from any direction. The giraffe's acute vision also lets it communicate through body language with other giraffes standing far away.

Or simply fall apart . . .

The **starfish** snaps off all its arms when frightened. Luckily, it is capable of regeneration. It grows new arms when it loses the old ones. In some cases, if a large piece breaks off a starfish, it can grow into a whole new creature.

Who Am I?

I am known for my terrible temper and will quickly charge anything that disturbs me. But if I am captured, I am easily tamed and become gentle and affectionate.

Am I . . .

a. a tiger?
b. a lion?
c. a polar bear?
d. a rhinoceros?

Friends or foes? Animals and people can be the best of friends or the worst of enemies. This Brain Buster is filled with off-the-wall info about amazing rescues. One astounding tale is complete hogwash. Are you up to the challenge of figuring out which one?

a. In 1938, 60 beaver colonies saved major highways, bridges, and hundreds of acres of valuable land in Stony Point, New York, from a raging flood. How'd they do it? By doing what beavers do best—they built dams that measured up to 600 feet long and 14 feet wide.

Believe It!   Not!

b. Monkeys took care of two-year-old John Ssebunya after he got lost in the jungle. The monkeys taught him to survive on fruits, nuts, and berries. After four years, John was found living among the monkeys and returned to his village in Uganda.

Believe It!   Not!

c. Lulu, a pig from Beaver Falls, Pennsylvania, saved the life of her owner. When Jo Altsaman suffered a massive heart attack, Lulu squeezed through the doggie door and ran into the road where she lay down and played dead. She got the attention of a young man whom she then led to Altsaman. He called 911, and Altsaman made it to the hospital in time for doctors to save her life!

Believe It!   Not!

d. Rats have an uncanny ability to find food. In 1993, a 14-year-old girl who was trapped on a deserted island in Indonesia was able to survive for three weeks on food she scavenged by following these rodents.

Believe It!   **Not!**

• •

BONUS QUESTION

What happened in 1891 when a sperm whale swallowed James Bartley?

a. Yuck! The whale spat him right back out. Bartley sustained only minor injuries and went on to become a renowned harpooner.

b. There were so many living fish swimming inside the whale's stomach that Bartley was able to survive for 42 days by using them for food.

c. The whale was badly injured by harpoons, and the next day, it was found dead, floating on the surface. Bartley was found in the whale's stomach, unconscious but still breathing.

5 Little Ones

Some mothers have lots of young at once . . .

The **nine-banded armadillo** always gives birth to quadruplets of the same sex. The babies are identical and are all formed from a single egg. The armadillo is the only mammal that regularly produces multiple young from one egg. Originally native to South America, this creature can now be found in Kansas, Louisiana, Oklahoma, and Texas.

The **tailless tenrec**, which is also known as the Madagascar hedgehog, regularly produces the largest litters of any mammal—as many as 32 babies at once. When threatened, a tenrec baby rubs together the bristles on its back. This produces an audible alarm signal that alerts its mother to the danger.

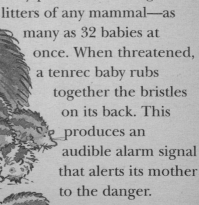

Others usually have one at a time . . .

A newborn **kangaroo** is typically just one inch long. Immediately after birth, this tiny blind creature crawls into its mother's pouch to nurse. Kangaroo mothers actually produce two different kinds of milk, allowing both newborn joeys (baby kangaroos) and an older sibling to nurse at the same time.

A newborn **panda** weighs just three to five ounces, about 1/900 of its mother's weight. Blind and hairless, the infant panda is constantly held and cradled by its mother for a week or more.

Who Am I?

My legs are as long at birth as they will be when I grow up.

Am I . . .

a. a horse?
b. a cat?
c. a koala?
d. a raccoon?

A **blue whale** infant gains weight at the rate of eight to ten pounds an hour. That's roughly 200 pounds or more a day! A newborn blue whale calf weighs about three tons and measures 23 to 27 feet long.

Some moms would do anything for their babies . . .

When a young **herring gull** taps the red mark on its mother's beak, she throws up whatever she has just eaten to feed it. Herring gulls will eat just about anything, from clams to dead animals to French fries. Some even scavenge food from garbage dumps, rather than looking for food at the seashore.

To make a soft, cozy home for its babies, the **white-eared honey-eater** steals the hair from passersby to line its nest. This songbird possesses a long, forked, tubular tongue. To feed, it sticks its tongue into flowers and sucks out the nectar and any small insects hiding inside.

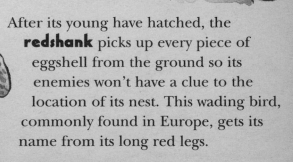

After its young have hatched, the **redshank** picks up every piece of eggshell from the ground so its enemies won't have a clue to the location of its nest. This wading bird, commonly found in Europe, gets its name from its long red legs.

The **golden eagle** attacks anything that approaches its nest—even helicopters and airplanes. This eagle lives in the mountains of Asia, Europe, and North America. Using sticks, it builds its nest in a tree or on a cliff. Every year, the golden eagle returns to the same nest to lay its eggs.

Who Am I?

After I produce my young, I often change my gender from male to female.

Am I . . .

a. a swordfish?
b. a crab?
c. a lobster?
d. an oyster?

An **octopus** protects her brood by starving herself. She stays with her eggs instead of looking for food. Most species of octopus lay their eggs in grapelike clusters, which they protect with their arms. The octopus is found in nearly all the oceans of the world.

And others would do anything to them . . .

The **water shrew** devours her babies if they don't follow her instructions. Some species of water shrew bear up to three litters a year, each one consisting of four to eight blind, hairless babies.

Some fathers care for their young . . .

At night, the male **ostrich** risks his life guarding his nest—even fighting lions to protect his newborn chicks. One male usually lives with a flock of three to five females, who lay their eggs in one communal nest. The nest can hold from 15 to 60 eggs. During the day, the females take turns watching the eggs.

Male **gorillas** band together to defend their young from poachers. Gorillas typically live in groups of five to ten individuals in the dense forests of central Africa. Full-grown adult males can weigh as much as 400 pounds and stand as tall as six feet. Mature males are called "silverback" gorillas after the wide band of silvery fur on their back.

The **sand grouse** flies as far as 50 miles a day to soak himself in water so that his young can drink from his feathers. A relative of the pigeon, the sand grouse lives in desert areas of Africa and Asia. When there are eggs in the nest, the grouse stays with them all day long to shade them from the hot sun. Once the chicks are hatched, the male heads to the nearest waterhole. He does this until his offspring are big enough to visit the waterhole themselves.

Who Am I?

I'm such a good father, I always hatch and feed my young.

Am I . . .

a. a crocodile?
b. a snake?
c. a platypus?
d. an emu?

The male **Darwin frog** hatches eggs in a pouch in his mouth. The female lays about 30 eggs on land, and the male guards them for two weeks before picking them up in his mouth. When the tadpoles lose their tails and become tiny frogs, they jump out of Daddy's mouth. Native to South America, this frog gets its name from Charles Darwin, the great naturalist who described their strange habits in the late 19th century. In Argentina, the Darwin frog is also known as a "vaquero."

Some parents feed their babies all day . . .

In searching for food, the **house wren** makes as many as 12,000 flights from its nest in a single day. This little songbird lays five to eight eggs in a clutch (or group) and can bear up to two clutches a year. The house wren will nest in birdhouses, trees—even in the pockets of clothes hung on a line to dry.

Some don't feed them at all . . .

The **cowbird** lays her eggs in the nests of other bird species and then takes off. Once the cowbird chick hatches, the other mother bird feeds the cowbird chick along with her own brood. Because of its behavior, the cowbird is known as a brood parasite.

Some parents take their babies everywhere . . .

Although a **pangolin** baby can walk a few days after birth, it rides on its mother's tail instead. If the mother feels threatened, she will curl her tail, with the baby on it, under her body. Any predators have to go through her before they can reach her baby.

The male **finfoot** carries his chicks in special pockets under his wings so he can fly with them. The finfoot is thought to be the only bird that carries its chicks in this way. Found in parts of Asia, Africa, Central and South America, these birds are also known as sun grebes.

Baby **wolf spiders** live on their mother's back until they are old enough to be on their own. This spider, which does not spin a web, also carries her eggs to protect them from predators.

And some leave them in daycare . . .

Who Am I?

I am three times longer than the egg I hatched from.

Am I . . .

a. an eagle chick?
b. a baby alligator?
c. an ostrich chick?
d. a cowbird chick?

Penguin parents leave their chicks in rookeries where they are watched over by other adult penguins. This allows both parents to go out looking for food. Penguins live only in the Southern Hemisphere.

Some babies take baths in mud . . .

A baby **elephant** takes mud baths to protect itself from sunburn. This also helps keep the animal cool and gets rid of pesky insects. Young elephants will often squirm around in the mud together and form a messy heap. Adults tend to pick the mud up with their trunks and fling it so that it lands on their bodies with a thwack.

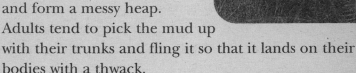

And some are afraid to swim . . .

When it gets old enough, a baby **seal** gets pushed into the water by its mother, who stays beside it until it loses its fear of the water. Newborn seals have a soft, downy coat that absorbs water. As they grow up, the young seals shed that coat and grow water-repellent fur. At that point, the young seals must learn to swim so they can hunt for food and escape from predators such as killer whales, polar bears, and sharks.

Some babies really stick together . . .

Baby **eels** travel in such tight formation, they often look like a ball of yarn. Some species of eel live in the ocean. Others inhabit freshwater. Some freshwater eels swim to the sea to lay their eggs. The eggs hatch and the eel larvae emerge. They grow and become elvers. The elvers eventually swim back to freshwater. Often they can be found in large groups at the mouths of rivers and streams.

Who Am I?

When I am a newborn, I leave no scent, so predators don't have a clue that I'm nearby.

Am I . . .

a. a skunk?
b. a tortoise?
c. a ferret?
d. a deer?

While others take up the whole nest . . .

Cuckoos, like cowbirds, are considered brood parasites. The mother cuckoo lays its egg in the nest of another bird species and leaves it to be hatched by the foster family. Sometimes the young cuckoo is bigger than its foster mother as well as its foster siblings. It competes with these siblings for food and may even push them out of the nest.

Ready to tackle the truth? You know the drill. Go for it!

a. Adult geese are highly protective of their goslings. When seven-year-old Megan Waltz of Newark, Delaware, hugged a young goose, a gaggle of geese held her captive in a tree for over 26 hours before firefighters were able to rescue her.

Believe It!   Not!

b. A cat, owned by A.W. Mitchell of Vancouver, British Columbia, nurtured 25 baby chicks.

Believe It!   Not!

c. A Canada goose and a Siberian husky from a farm in Yakima, Washington, are BFFs—best friends forever. Not only does the goose sleep in the doghouse and share the dog's food, but it will face off against other dogs that try to enter the doghouse.

Believe It!   Not!

d. Golden Duke, a rooster owned by O.J. Plomeson of Luverne, Minnesota, could pull Plomeson's baby daughter in a carriage down Main Street!

Believe It!   Not!

BONUS QUESTION

What made Koko, a gorilla who understands the meaning of at least 500 words in sign language, cry for two days?

a. She was told that her pet cat had died.

b. She was told she had to move to another zoo.

c. She realized two young boys were using sign language to insult her.

d. She was bullied by an older and bigger gorilla.

Ripley's Believe It or Not! Brain Buster

POP QUIZ

It's not over yet. How much do you remember about World's Weirdest Critters? It's time to test your knowledge. Ready to tackle the toughest Ripley's Brain Buster yet? Circle your answers and give yourself five points for each question you answer correctly.

1. Which one of the following is NOT something animals do with their tongues?
a. Suck nectar from flowers.
b. Catch ants.
c. Clean the lint out of their navels.

2. Hippo sweat looks like blood, but it's really . . .
a. a kind of skin conditioner.
b. a mucouslike coating that protects hippos from poisonous plants.
c. a slime that makes it difficult for predators to attack them.
The hippos are so slippery, attackers hit their sides and slide right off.

3. If a crocodile loses a tooth, it just grows back. It can lose and regrow up to 300 teeth in its lifetime.

Believe It!   **Not!**

4. The ruffed grouse grows wings every year right before winter so it can fly south.

Believe It!   **Not!**

5. Which oddity is false?
a. The cormorant can eat three times its weight in fish each day.
b. A bat can eat over 3,000 insects in one night.
c. A Siberian brown bear will only eat fish heads.
d. A hummingbird drinks the nectar from 1,000 flowers every day.

6. Which one don't you believe?
a. A polar bear can smell its prey up to 100 miles away.
b. A coyote can hear a mouse moving under one foot of snow.
c. The green-backed heron catches insects and uses them as bait to lure fish.
d. The trapdoor spider builds a burrow with a trapdoor and waits for dinner to drop by.

7. What does a hummingbird use to build its nest?

a. The stems of dead flowers.

b. Spiderwebs.

c. Anything it can find—including straw, weeds, and even garbage.

8. Which one is NOT a way that animals help one another?

a. Birds pick and clean the teeth of crocodiles.

b. Birds eat ticks off a rhino's back.

c. Birds balance vertically on water while schools of small fish remove dirt from their feathers.

9. Which is NOT a way that animals communicate with one another?

a. A language of sounds similar to Japanese.

b. Dancing.

c. Low-frequency sounds.

d. Electrical signals.

10. Flying dragons can glide up to 150 feet!

Believe It!   **Not!**

11. Prairie dogs identify one another by kissing. They press their teeth against one another's faces.

Believe It!   **Not!**

12. Which is false?

a. Some moths are able to jam a bat's sonar so the bat can't find them.

b. The California roadrunner captures snakes by luring them into a pit using a trail of cactus spines.

c. The lyrebird can impersonate the songs and cries of other birds.

d. The sea cucumber defends itself by "throwing up" its own digestive system.

13. What does the houbara bustard do when it's being chased by a hawk?

a. Sprays the hawk's eyes and feathers with a thick sticky fluid that blinds and disables it.

b. Retaliates with a foul-smelling spray.

c. Squirts blood from its eyes.

d. Curls up into a ball.

14. A female octopus protects her brood by hiding them inside conch shells.

Believe It!　　　**Not!**

15. Baby seals have to be taught not to be afraid of the water.

Believe It!　　　**Not!**

Answer Key

Chapter One

Who Am I?

Page 6:   **d.** turtle
Page 8:   **a.** Manx
Page 10:   **b.** squirrel
Page 12:   **c.** earthworm
Page 15:   **c.** lobster
Page 16:   **d.** platypus
Brain Buster: **c** is false.
Bonus Question: **a.**

Chapter Two

Who Am I?

Page 20:   **a.** parrot
Page 23:   **d.** pelican eel
Page 24:   **b.** fish (Indian climbing perch)
Page 26:   **b.** crab
Page 28:   **c.** oyster
Page 30:   **a.** giant panda
Brain Buster: **b** is false.
Bonus Question: **c.**

Chapter Three

Who Am I?

Page 34: **b.** mockingbird
Page 36: **a.** ant (magnetic ant)
Page 38: **c.** ant (Amazon ant)
Page 40: **d.** owl (burrowing owl)
Brain Buster: c is false.
Bonus Question: b.

Chapter Four

Who Am I?

Page 44: **b.** sheep
Page 46: **d.** monkey (Barbary macaque)
Page 49: **a.** cowbird
Page 50: **c.** komodo dragon
Page 52: **d.** octopus (blue-ringed octopus)
Page 54: **b.** caiman
Page 56: **a.** chameleon
Page 59: **c.** bison
Page 60: **d.** rhinoceros
Brain Buster: d is false.
Bonus Question: c.

Chapter Five

Who Am I?

Page 64:   **a.** horse

Page 66:   **d.** oyster

Page 68:   **d.** emu

Page 70:   **b.** baby alligator

Page 72:   **d.** deer

Brain Buster: a is false.

Bonus Question: a.

Pop Quiz

1. **c.**
2. **a.**
3. **Believe It!**
4. **Not!**
5. **a.**
6. **a.**
7. **b.**
8. **c.**
9. **a.**
10. **Believe It!**
11. **Believe It!**
12. **b.**
13. **a.**
14. **Not!**
15. **Believe It!**

What's Your Ripley's Rank?

Ripley's Scorecard

Congrats! Now it's time to rate your Ripley's knowledge. Are you an Extreme Expert or a Ripley's Rookie? Check out the answers in the answer key and use this page to keep track of how many trivia questions you've answered correctly. Then add 'em up and find out how you rate.

Here's the scoring breakdown—give yourself:

★ **10 points** for every **Who Am I?** you answered correctly;

★ **20 points** for every fiction you spotted in the **Ripley's Brain Busters**;

★ **10** for every **Bonus Question** you answered right and;

★ **5** for every **Pop Quiz** question you answered correctly.

Here's a tally sheet:

Number of **Who Am I?** questions
answered correctly: _____ x 10 = _____

Number of **Ripley's Brain Busters**
questions answered correctly: _____ x 20 = _____

Number of **Bonus Questions**
answered correctly: _____ x 10 = _____

Chapter Total: _____

Write your totals for each chapter and the Pop Quiz section in the spaces below. Then add them up to get your FINAL SCORE. Your FINAL SCORE decides how you rate.

Chapter One Total: _____

Chapter Two Total: _____

Chapter Three Total _____

Chapter Four Total: _____

Chapter Five Total: _____

Pop Quiz Total: _____

FINAL SCORE: _____

525—301
Extreme Expert

Your Ripley's know-how is top-notch. No one can pull anything over on you. You just don't fall for tricks. You know that truth can be stranger than fiction—and you like it that way. Your sense for the strange, bent for the bizarre, and talent for spotting the truth in the absurd are hard to believe. And you wow your friends with your grasp of the freakish and outlandish. Maybe you have discovered a rare Ripley's oddity of your own—or maybe it's time to add yourself to the ranks of the truly amazing. You're superhuman—**Believe It!**

300–201
Best of the Bizarre

Your Ripley's know-how ranks high. You have an impressive eye for the bizarre, but you're no know-it-all. Your ability to spot a hoax is uncanny, but even the best get stumped once in a while. Cut yourself some slack— the line between truth and fiction isn't always so easy to figure out. Trust your instincts—and keep it up, superstar!

200–101
Amazing Amateur

You're rising in the ranks, but tales of sea cucumbers throwing up their insides are more than you can deal with. You can separate the more obvious fictions from the facts, but when it comes to the Brain Busters, your sense for the strange is out of whack. Chin up! Give it another try—you've got shocking potential.

100–0
Ripley's Rookie

The odd, bizarre, and super-strange are just not your style. It's too much to think about. You'd prefer to strain your brain on less amazing tales. You stick to the everyday, the concrete, the norm—and you're not apologizing for it. That's cool. But remember, the world is a weird and wacky place. And sometimes the truth really is stranger than fiction.

Photo Credits

Ripley Entertainment and the editors of this book wish to thank the following photographers, agents, and other individuals for permission to use and reprint the following photographs in this book. Any photographs included in this book that are not acknowledged below are property of the Ripley Archives. Great effort has been made to obtain permission from the owners of all materials included in this book. Any errors that may have been made are unintentional and will gladly be corrected in future printings if notice is sent to Ripley Entertainment, 5728 Major Boulevard, Orlando, Florida 32819.

Black & White Photos

5 Anteater; 7 Wolf; 8 Sphynx; 11 Walrus;
19 Bat, Pheasant; 22 Koala; 24 Sea Snake;
27 Polar Bear; 30 Moray Eel;
34 Hummingbird; 39 Hermit Crab;
47 Gorilla; 48 Cranes; 50 Frilled Lizard;
52 Sea Cucumber; 53 Tiger; 55 Porcupine;
57 Meerkats; 60 Giraffe; 64 Kangaroos;
69 House Wren; 70 Penguins; 71 Baby
Elephant/Copyright © 2001 Ripley
Entertainment and its licensors

6 Tuatara/Steven Holt/Aigrette Stockpix

16 Aardvark; 23 Peregrine Falcon;
60 Starfish/PhotoDisc

21 Hummingbird; 66 Octopus/CORBIS

25 Elephant Seals/Dennis Sheridan

26 Osprey; 33 Lion/EyeWire

29 Trapdoor Spider; 36 Water Spider/David
Glynne Fox

45 Red-capped Mangabey/Samantha Smith/
Yerkes Regional Primate Research Center

46 Prairie Dogs/W. Perry/CORBIS

51 Crested Bellbird/Kevin Roberts

56 Thorny Devil/Gerry Ellis/Minden Pictures

58 Marsupial Mouse/John Eisenberg

68 Sand Grouse/Keith Sloan/Nature Portfolio

Color Insert

Aardvark/PhotoDisc

Blue-ringed Octopus/George Grall
© National Aquarium in Baltimore

Emu/Bob Ford/Nature Portfolio

Kiwi/Tui De Roy/Minden Pictures

Lyrebird/J. Warham/Vireo

Frilled Lizard; Meerkats; Moray Eel; Pangolin;
Puffin; Sphynx/Copyright © 2001 Ripley
Entertainment and its licensors

Okapi/Brent Huffman/The Ultimate
Ungulate Page/www.ultimateungulate.com

Owl Butterfly/Doug Wechsler/Vireo

Parrotfish/Fred Bavendam/Minden Pictures

Sea Cucumber/Jeffrey L. Rotman/CORBIS

Spicebush Swallowtail Caterpillar/Jason D.
Weintraub/Aurelian Entographics

Thorny Devil/Frans Lanting/Minden Pictures

Textures and Backgrounds/CORBIS

Trapdoor Spiders; Water Spider/David
Glynne Fox

Tuatara/Steven Holt/Aigrette Stockpix

Vampire Bat/Gary Braasch/CORBIS

Wolf Fish/Peter Auster and Paul Donaldson,
National Undersea Research Center,
University of Connecticut

If you enjoyed **World's Weirdest Critters**, get ready for

 **Creepy Stuff**

We are taught to believe in only those things we can see, hear, smell, taste, or touch. But then . . .

How did Hubert Pearce correctly guess every card in the ESP tests he was given at Duke University?

Why do police ask psychics for help in locating missing persons?

How can some people predict the exact moment when they will die?

Why do the ghosts of people who died long ago sometimes pop up in the homes they once lived in?

You'll read about these things and more in **Creepy Stuff**. But be warned: Do not read **Creepy Stuff** before you go to sleep— unless, of course, you're not afraid of things that go bump in the night!